A MIND OF A KIND

PRITI SINGH

Made with ♥ on the Notion Press Platform
www.notionpress.com

Dedicated to the fighter in me. You go gurl!

Contents

Contents

Preface

I WROTE
A BOOK!!!

Hey everyone, my name is Priti, and here's me writing yet another book. If you're reading this, it is either because

1. You know me
2. Or because you don't

Either way, I'm glad you're here. Thank you for getting your hands on this book. This book is a refined version of my very first book that I wrote at nineteen. Since I'm a year older, I aim to provide more insights and knowledge. This book can be read by adults and even adolescents willing to conquer their minds and live a meaningful and worthwhile life. Although the book is sequential, you don't have to read it like that. You can read it in whichever way you find it helpful.

This book talks about my life but concentrates more on past the age of fourteen. It talks about how I've lived a life with several mental illnesses, survived suicide attempts, and emerged to be a happier and more content person in life. I want to tell people that sometimes it's going to be you up against your hormones and sometimes, even against your mind.

Life isn't fair. We don't get rainbows, and unicorns, and glitter, and sparkles. We get problems and hardships at times and we've got to learn to face them. That's how we get stronger. I began fighting my mind at the mere age of eight, and yes, that is early. But I had to do it and I continue doing it even today, every day.

Schizophrenia is something beautiful and I'll try my best to align your thoughts with mine by the time you read the entire book.

I am no expert and I don't claim to be one. But what I've gone through has helped me learn lots of things. I'm just putting an effort into sharing what I learned with you, my friend.

So, what is schizophrenia? Schizophrenia is a severe mental condition that basically means a split mind. How can a mind be split? Well, think of it like this. The person dealing with schizophrenia lives in two or more worlds but only one of them is real. The best and worst part is, you can't even tell the difference! Imagination can be the worst and biggest enemy of a person dealing with schizophrenia. But, did you know, people who have schizophrenia are damn creative. Can you see the positive side of it already? They see, and hear things that are not real. Sometimes, they can taste, feel, and smell unreal things too. These are called hallucinations. So basically, there is no real stimulus. Hallucinations can feel very real and it can get difficult to distinguish between what is real and what is not. They also have false beliefs called delusions (more commonly known as delulu, thanks to Instagram). They might believe that they have superpowers or that people can read their minds, which is not really true and merely impossible. However, their beliefs are so strong that their minds are fixated on those delusions. These are two common symptoms of schizophrenia. Alongside this, people have distorted and disorganized thinking. There is no cure to this illness and it is chronic.

There are different kinds of schizophrenia. The one that I was diagnosed with is paranoid schizophrenia. Paranoid schizophrenia involves experiences of paranoia. People may believe that everyone is plotting against them and may trust very few people. In my case, I don't drink anybody else's water because who knows if there is poison in it.

Schizophrenia does not have a cure. However, some therapies and treatments may help the person cope with his/her symptoms.

We'll learn more as we read through. So, are you ready? Let's go!

Wholeheartedly,
Priti
Singh ♥

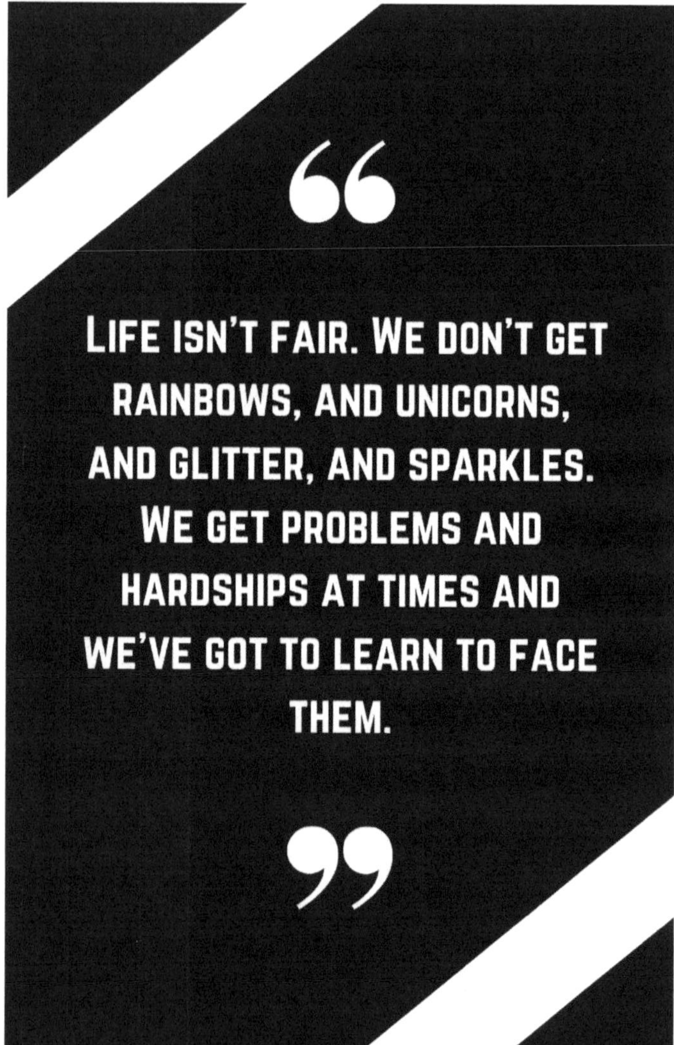
LIFE ISN'T FAIR. WE DON'T GET RAINBOWS, AND UNICORNS, AND GLITTER, AND SPARKLES. WE GET PROBLEMS AND HARDSHIPS AT TIMES AND WE'VE GOT TO LEARN TO FACE THEM.

Acknowledgements

This book is about how to stand strong even with an illness that brings you down. Certain people (and dogs) let me lean on them when I was being pulled down. And to those special ones, I want to say thank you.

I thank my mom and dad for tirelessly providing me with everything I need and supporting me for all these 20 years. I thank my brother and sister-in-law for guiding me on my way to independence and for making me see how real life can get. I also thank my aunt, uncle, and close cousins who were always ready to help me and my mom when I was amid horrible episodes and for filling in my dad's absence.

I thank my teachers from Ryan and Deens- Rose Mary Ma'am (JD), Sudipa Ma'am, Sunitha Ma'am, Sweta Ma'am, Archana Ma'am, Asha Ma'am, Priyanka Ma'am, Charlotte Ma'am, Jeyasri Ma'am, Rupa ma'am, Sonia Ma'am, and Neeta Ma'am for being there for me and helping me with my coursework.

I thank my principals- Vidya Ma'am and Chandra Ma'am- for understanding my situation and helping me through high school.

I am grateful to my college management for encouraging and guiding me toward success.

I extend my special thanks to Minnu Ma'am, Augustin Sir, Arunima Ma'am, and Eldhose Sir for taking care of me at college and making me feel like I belong. I thank my special friends- Sneha, Manu, Dhananjay, Dixit, and Nishchay. I am grateful for my awesome seniors and wonderful juniors who support and take care of me. I wouldn't have made it to my final year without all of you.

Apart from those mentioned above, I thank all my friends and teachers who have extended their support to me.

Thank you doctors and therapists for making me realize that I'm so much more than my illness. Your support has been invaluable.

To every reader reading this, I hope this book is helpful to you and gives you something good to take away.

JUST FYI

CHAPTER ONE

Schizophrenia in a Nutshell

Schizophrenia is a mental illness that has an impact on how a person thinks, feels, and acts. It often causes a break from reality, which can scare and confuse those who have it as well as their loved ones.

Schizophrenia shows up in the late teens or early twenties. While it's not as common as some other mental health issues affecting about 1 in 100 people, it changes lives. We don't know what causes schizophrenia yet, but studies point to a mix of genes, brain chemicals, and life experiences playing a role.

Schizophrenia has a range of symptoms, which doctors group into positive negative, and cognitive categories. Positive symptoms include behaviours that healthy people don't experience, like hallucinations and delusions. During hallucinations, a person might see, hear, or feel things that aren't real. Delusions are strong beliefs that don't match reality. Thought disorders, which show up as jumbled thinking, and movement disorders, which can make someone move a lot or move at all also fall under positive symptoms.

Negative symptoms show disruptions in normal emotional and behavioural functioning. People might show a "flat affect," where they express less emotion through their face or voice tone. They may also find it hard to enjoy everyday activities, struggle to start and keep up with activities, and speak less.

Cognitive symptoms, while often subtle and detectable through specific tests, include problems with executive functioning such as trouble understanding and using information to make decisions. Issues with attention and working memory—using information right after learning it—are also common cognitive symptoms in schizophrenia.

Schizophrenia has many causes. Genes play a big part; the disorder often runs in families, but having a relative with schizophrenia doesn't mean you'll get it too. Brain chemistry and structure also matter. Imbalances in brain chemicals like dopamine and glutamate and differences in brain structure might contribute to the disorder. Outside factors can increase the risk of developing schizophrenia too. These include viral infections before birth poor nutrition, and very stressful events.

Living with schizophrenia poses big challenges, but many people still enjoy good lives with proper care and help. Drugs antipsychotics, can lessen the strength of psychotic symptoms. Cognitive-behavioral therapy (CBT) helps people cope with symptoms and boosts their quality of life. Support networks, like family, friends, and group meetings, make a big difference. They offer understanding and patience, which improve the well-being of those who have schizophrenia. Also, a healthy way of life through regular workouts good food, and staying away from drugs and booze can lead to better overall health and symptom control.

Even though we've made big strides in figuring out and treating schizophrenia, lots of myths and wrong ideas still hang around, which leads to stigma and confusion. One myth you hear a lot is that schizophrenia means having split personalities, but that's not true. Schizophrenia is about having a hard time telling what's real from what's not rather than having multiple personalities. Another damaging myth is that people with schizophrenia are dangerous by nature. In fact, most folks with schizophrenia aren't violent and are more likely to be hurt by others than to hurt someone else. The wrong idea that bad parenting causes schizophrenia ignores the complex mix of things that play a part in this illness.

Although schizophrenia has no cure progress in medical science and better knowledge of the disorder have boosted the outlook for patients. Taking action and getting ongoing help can make a big difference in controlling symptoms and improving life quality.

Schizophrenia doesn't define a person. With understanding good treatment, and strong support networks, people with schizophrenia can live worthwhile satisfying lives. Understanding schizophrenia is key to reducing stigma and offering the right support to those affected. If you or someone you know shows signs of schizophrenia getting help from a doctor can lead to early action and better handling of the illness. This can help to create a more positive and rewarding life.

my Laif

CHAPTER TWO

First Signs and my Early Experiences

As a child, I missed having two parents. All my friends lived with both their parents, whereas I only lived with my mom. It wasn't that I didn't have a dad, I just lived away from him. His job required him to work abroad. I felt very lonely, obviously. I cried a lot, even for the smallest of things. Due to this, I didn't have any friends. I was often the last option for kids to call me out to play. At home, it was just me, my mom, and my brother who is nine years older than me.

Time flew and my brother was giving his entrances for college. I was 8 years old at that time. I was scared of just one thing and that was if my brother got into a college that wasn't in the same city, he'd have to move and I'd be left alone. This fear of mine turned true when my brother announced with joy that he got into the National Institute of Technology, Surathkal. Don't get me wrong, I was very happy for my brother but tears rolled down my cheeks as we dropped him off at college.

A few days after we dropped my brother, I went through something I had never gone through. I was sitting in math class at school and I felt my heart thumping. My palms began to sweat and I wasn't able to breathe properly. However, the severity of these symptoms was minimal. I didn't say anything to my friends or my teacher and waited for it to pass. I went home and pretended that nothing ever happened. A couple of months later, I was at home doing normal eight-year-old things when I felt the amount of air around me decrease. My heart began racing and I could barely breathe. I was trying to explain what was happening to my mom when it all went pitch black. I went unconscious. My mom, and one of our family friends, drove me to the nearest hospital. There we found out what I was going through was called anxiety and that the major cause of it was loneliness. Soon enough, I found myself thrown into painting, skating, swimming, and dance classes. This was my mom's attempt to keep me busy so I didn't have time to think about how I didn't have anyone.

Fast forward to middle school, I had another panic attack in 7th grade. The school called my mom and asked her to pick me up. As I grew older, my anxiety worsened. To keep myself busy, one of my close teachers, Ms. Rose Mary asked me to fill out the nomination form for the student council. And so, I did. I gave my speech and even got elected as the deputy health minister of my school. Everything was going well, I was doing my duty fine, but as the stressors around me increased, I started having panic attacks every day. They weren't just panic attacks; they were the worst kind of panic attacks where I couldn't even move. I was once locked inside the restroom for an entire period (30 minutes) because I had an attack and I couldn't call for help.

The episodes got so bad that my parents decided I needed help. We visited a general physician. She was genuinely concerned and suggested we visit a psychiatrist, so we did. Then I was diagnosed with acute Generalized Anxiety Disorder (GAD). I was put on a few basic medications. I was very distressed and began self-harm and I went down a deep, deep never-ending hole.

Soon, I was transferred to NIMHANS and that's when my treatment actually began. At NIMHANS, they don't focus on the diagnosis, rather they focus on the patient's experiences and troubles. The doctors said that I was dissociating and showed signs of psychosis. I would often feel that everybody was talking about me. I felt people were going to harm me. I also made a few friends who weren't real. I would speak with them for hours. I was constantly frightened and saw things that didn't exist. The voices just got louder with time. I was hospitalized thrice in the adolescent psychiatry unit. I made a few friends and I had a great time there. Those friends understood me because even they were going through something.

A few months later, I was diagnosed with anorexia. I believed I was too fat whereas I was actually on the lower side of the BMI scale. Nobody was successful in convincing me that I was not fat. But numbers weighed upon my head and I began weighing myself even when I was in the hospital. I played badminton inside the ward with table tennis bats, and I did whatever I could to burn calories. And then I became underweight and had to be tubed at a hospital. So basically, I had a lot of things going on. Depression, anxiety, hallucinations, delusions, paranoia, and my eating disorder troubled me so much that I wanted to quit it all and die. I made a few attempts too but thankfully, I was unsuccessful.

CHAPTER THREE

DEALING WITH THE DIAGNOSIS

Not very long after my eighteenth birthday, I was diagnosed with paranoid schizophrenia with dissociative episodes. That was a daunting fact for me to digest. However, I was glad we had come to some conclusion after all these years. Having a clear picture was better than having a vague one and that was possible because of my great doctors at NIMHANS and Cadabam's hospital.

But, I'll be very honest with you. It didn't take me long to accept my diagnosis. Acceptance is the most important thing in order to know yourself and function. Soon, my friends and relatives found out and they were very supportive.

I began my research about the medications I took. I was already studying psychology at college. I was in my first semester when I was diagnosed. I had to know about what was happening to me and so I began studying more about it. The only way to be in control is to know what is happening to my body and what the medications I took did to my brain.

Since the age of fourteen, I had to keep my lithium levels in check and under control as lithium in excess can be toxic. I had blood drawn every few weeks to monitor the levels and that continues even today. I then studied more and more about my illness and came to terms with it. I also learned that when neurons in your brain fire too fast, you have convulsions. That was exactly what was happening to me. I slowly learned a little every day and today if someone asks me, "What exactly is wrong with you?", I can answer confidently.

At college, I had episodes on a daily basis but Minnu Ma'am and Augustin Sir took special care of me, tirelessly. They were literally just a call away. I mean the literal meaning of 'literally' when I say this. They teach psychology at my college and they play a major role in my journey towards growth and acceptance.

When people asked, I wasn't ashamed to tell them about my illness. Only 1% of people in the world are affected by schizophrenia. One in many people suffer from this illness. I don't know about the suffering part, but I am proud to say that I am one in many, even if it's an illness. I mean, it is just an illness, right?

For the most part, when people ask me about who my role model is, I often give thought to people with schizophrenia who have done something with their lives. I realized that I didn't know anyone like that. There may be people but I didn't know them. So I didn't really have a role model. In fact, I aim to be a role model for people with schizophrenia. So many people including my teachers have told me that I am an inspiration to them and I would say that's a good thing for me. People may call my brain defective but I feel that is my biggest strength.

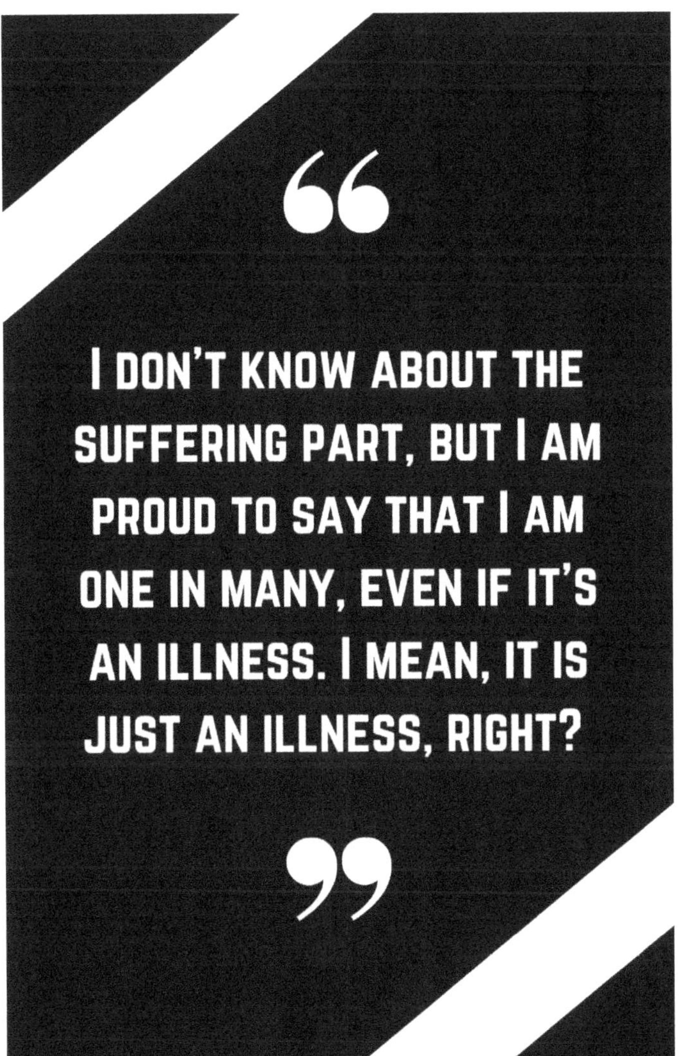
I DON'T KNOW ABOUT THE SUFFERING PART, BUT I AM PROUD TO SAY THAT I AM ONE IN MANY, EVEN IF IT'S AN ILLNESS. I MEAN, IT IS JUST AN ILLNESS, RIGHT?

CHAPTER FOUR

HIGH SCHOOL CHALLENGES

High school was a tumultuous time for me, because of both academic pressures and the intense struggle with my mental health. One of the most significant and horrifying experiences I had happened when I was in the 10th grade. It was a day that started just like any other but quickly spiralled into a profound crisis that shaped my understanding of my condition and the strength of the support system around me.

It was a typical afternoon in Sudipa Ma'am's class. She was one of my favourite teachers. She was very encouraging and always had a cheerful attitude. As she taught, I tried to focus on the class, but I soon began to feel uneasy. Suddenly, I saw a girl standing outside the classroom window. She wasn't a student from our school; her presence was unfamiliar and unsettling. I knew immediately that she wasn't real—a hallucination, one of the many that interrupted my daily life.

I was filled with panic. I felt an overwhelming urge to escape the vision that haunted me. Without thinking, I left the class abruptly, ignoring the confused looks from my classmates and the concerned call from Sudipa Ma'am. I sprinted down the hallway and made my way to the second floor, my heart pounding in my chest.

In my panic, I climbed the railing intending to jump off. The rational part of my mind was drowned out by the fear and confusion the hallucination had induced. As I stood there, on the edge, two boys noticed me. Their quick thinking saved my life. They called for help, and within seconds, teachers arrived, pulling me down from the railing and leading me to the infirmary. I don't remember exactly but I know for sure that Rose Mary, Archana , and Sudipa ma'am were there for sure. There were a few other teachers to whom I'm grateful.

The school infirmary was a quiet space away from the chaos of the corridors. As I sat there, trying to calm my racing thoughts, the teachers contacted my mother. When she arrived, I could see the worry on her face. The incident was a sharp reminder of how fragile my mental state was and how much support I needed to deal with these difficult times.

The next day, my principal, Vidya Ma'am called my mother in for a meeting. She was compassionate and understanding, emphasizing the importance of my well-being over my attendance. She suggested that I stay home until I felt better, a decision I was incredibly grateful for. This support from my school played an immense role in giving me the time and space I needed to recover.

For the next few months, I stayed home, focusing on my mental health and slowly rebuilding my strength. When I finally felt ready to return to school, it was a fresh start, but not without its challenges.

My mother accompanied me to school every day, waiting in the office while I attended classes. This arrangement provided me with a sense of security, knowing that she was nearby if I needed her. Most days, I could only manage a half-day of classes before my symptoms became too overwhelming. Yet, my mother stayed in the school office throughout the day, ready to support me whenever I needed to leave early.

The understanding and accommodation from my teachers and the principal were invaluable. They never made me feel like a burden or an inconvenience. Instead, they showed genuine concern for my well-being and went out of their way to ensure I had the support I needed.

Returning to school was not easy. Each day was a battle with my mind, and there were many moments of doubt and fear. However, with my mother's support and the compassionate understanding of my school, I slowly began to find my footing.

The incident in Sudipa Ma'am's class was a turning point, a moment that taught me the importance of mental health awareness and support. It was a reminder that even in our darkest moments, we are not alone, and with the right support, we can find our way back to the light.

After my return to school, every day was filled with ups and downs and presented its own set of challenges. The process of reintegration was slow and fraught with moments of anxiety and self-doubt. I often wondered if I would ever be able to live a "normal" life again. But with every small victory, I gained a little more confidence in myself and my ability to manage my symptoms.

My peers' reactions were mixed. Some were curious, some were supportive, and some distanced themselves, unsure of how to interact with me. This was another layer of challenge—navigating social dynamics while dealing with my mental health. I learned to communicate openly with my close friends, explaining my condition and what I was going through. This openness helped build a support network among my peers, even if it was small.

My teachers played a crucial role. They made accommodations for me, such as allowing extra time for assignments and providing a quiet space for me to retreat to if needed. This flexibility was essential in helping me cope with the academic pressures of high school. They treated me with kindness and respect, which made a world of difference. It showed me that I was valued not just as a student, but as a person.

I then joined my pre-university college. There, I met some really nice teachers and friends. The school counsellor, Charlotte Ma'am became an important figure in my life during this time. Regular sessions with her helped me process my experiences and develop coping strategies. She taught me techniques for managing anxiety and recognizing the early signs of a psychotic episode. This proactive approach helped me feel more in control of my mental health and less like a victim of my circumstances. Here too, I had an amazing principal, Chandra Ma'am, and some really supportive teachers like Priyanka, Jeyasri, Rupa, and Neeta Ma'am, among others.

Over time, I began to rebuild my academic life. I set small, achievable goals for myself and celebrated each accomplishment, no matter how minor it seemed. This approach helped me regain a sense of purpose and direction

As I gradually increased my time at school, my mother started to step back, allowing me to become more independent. This transition was challenging but necessary. It was a testament to the progress I had made and the resilience I had developed

The support of my school community extended beyond just my immediate circle. There were teachers and staff members who might not have known the specifics of my situation but still offered a smile or a kind word. These small gestures of kindness made a significant impact. They reminded me that compassion and understanding could be found in unexpected places.

Reflecting on this period, I realize how crucial it was for my schools to have a culture of empathy and support. It wasn't just the policies or accommodations that made a difference, but the attitudes and behaviours of the people around me. Their willingness to understand and support me played a significant role in my journey towards stability.

High school, with all its challenges, was a pivotal time in my life. It tested my limits and forced me to confront my mental health head-on. But it also showed me the strength of my spirit and the incredible power of a supportive community. The lessons I learned during this time have stayed with me and continue to guide me in my ongoing journey with schizophrenia.

The incident in Sudipa Ma'am's class, though terrifying, ultimately became a catalyst for change (She taught chemistry. Pun Intended!). It was a wake-up call that highlighted the urgent need for support and understanding. It taught me that seeking help is not a sign of weakness but a courageous step towards healing.

This chapter of my life is a testament to resilience, the importance of support, and the strong belief that things can get better. It is a reminder to anyone facing similar challenges that they are not alone, and that with patience, support, and self-compassion, it is possible to deal with even the most daunting obstacles.

CHAPTER FIVE

A Typical Day in My Life

I wake up and watch the sunrise. Nope, that's all lies.

My actual day goes something like this. On a day that I have somewhere to be, and that somewhere is mostly college, I wake up around 7 o'clock. This is on a good day when I've slept the night. On days when I get no sleep or very little sleep, I'm usually up till 6. Then, I sleep for an hour until 7. Sometimes I have disturbances throughout the night and can barely sleep. And on some nights, it's all good. By disturbances, I'm referring to hallucinations. I can sometimes see people in my mirror and hear voices. The voices may be of a single person, or of two or more people. Sometimes, they're not even talking to me. They talk among themselves. Either way, it is quite disturbing. The more I try and ignore it, the louder it gets. This usually happens when I don't take my pills at night. But it can happen even if I do take my meds. If anything such happens, I always have my mom who stays with me throughout the night and takes care of me.

Anyway, once I'm up, I get ready for the day and mostly skip breakfast. I then take my pills which are carefully arranged in my Monday to Sunday pill box which is refilled by mom every Sunday. She does the job of cutting my pills if they need any cutting and placing them according to my dosage. Next, I take Shiro, my dog, for a walk, if I have the time. Otherwise, he plays around in the backyard. After that, it's almost 8 and I leave for college. My mom drops me to college every day. I don't take the college bus because I can dissociate anywhere, anytime and things are mostly unpredictable. However, I sometimes go on my own using Uber. That has only started recently, though.

I reach college around 8:30 and go for my first class. I spend my day with my awesome friends and teachers. During my first semester, I had episodes every single day. But gradually, they reduced in frequency. Whenever I have any kind of disturbance, my friends who are majorly juniors and seniors take care of me. At this point, they know how to deal with my episodes. I have some really supportive teachers who prioritize me and attend to me. So, going to college is genuinely not an issue as I feel like I belong there. If it gets too out of hand, my friends call my mom and she picks me up. Or they give me an SOS clonazepam which reduces the intensity of my episodes.

If I have a free class, you'll either find me in the psychology lab, or the media lab. These are my niche. We have a live streaming room in the media lab which is a small room with an AC in it. I love spending my time there with the AC turned on at 16 degrees. I always attend my seniors' or juniors' classes when I have a free hour. I am unofficially in my third year along with my seniors.

During the lunch break, my friends and I go outside to have lunch. Trust me when I say this, we're late almost every time for the next class. I attend the last two classes and my mom picks me up at 3:30. I reach home around

4:15 and freshen up by 4:30. I then sleep. What happens on a lot of days is I sleep till the next morning. My mind sometimes shuts down and I'm off till the next day. So I skip my meds that day which further becomes an issue for the next day. But if that's not the case, I get up around 6 or 6:30 PM. I then make myself some tea or coffee and sit with my academics. Sometimes my aunt comes over or I go to her place so I have my tea there.

I usually have dissociative episodes at home during which I sometimes act like a child. During this time, I am totally disconnected from reality and once I am back to normal, I can't seem to remember anything. My mom usually stays by my side throughout my episode and comforts me.

Next, I take Shiro for a walk, have some dinner, and take my pills after doing a lot of drama because I don't like swallowing such huge pills. I mean, it gets very uncomfortable. Then I talk to my dad and brother over the phone and attempt to sleep.

Now note that throughout the day I have voices either telling me what I'm doing or telling me what to do. But, after all these years, I have built up enough resilience to manage them and continue my work. I have to note my complaints and disturbances so I can tell my doctor when I visit him.

There is no such thing as a perfect day. Every day I get to experience the creative creations of my mind aka my hallucinations.

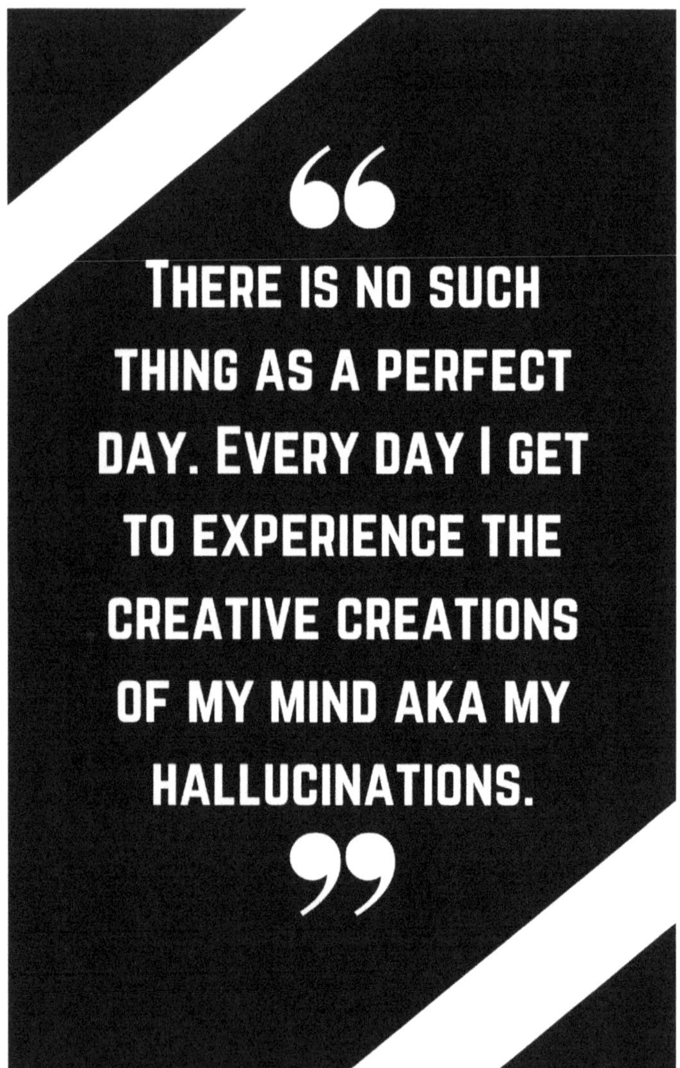
"
THERE IS NO SUCH
THING AS A PERFECT
DAY. EVERY DAY I GET
TO EXPERIENCE THE
CREATIVE CREATIONS
OF MY MIND AKA MY
HALLUCINATIONS.
"

CHAPTER SIX

OVERCOMING STIGMA AND SHARING MY STORY

Stigma has always been a shadow lurking behind. When I was first diagnosed, I quickly realized that the illness wasn't just about managing symptoms; it was also about battling the misconceptions and prejudice that came along with it. Sharing my story and confronting stigma head-on became an integral part of my growing process. I hope my experiences can inspire others to do the same.

The first time I encountered stigma was when I had a panic attack at school and some people commented, "It's just for attention". I was actually more shocked than hurt because people who were educated had very little understanding of what mental illness is. That's not just it. I have had people tell me, "But you don't *look* crazy". Even people who were very close to me said things like that. I was honestly surprised to see how little people knew about mental health and mental illnesses. People with schizophrenia are not crazy; they are creative and powerful.

The media isn't any helpful. The media portrays people who have schizophrenia as violent and outrageous. They portray them as harmful and totally disconnected from reality. That is not how it is, to be honest. This portrayal adds to the fear and misconceptions of people around me making it more difficult for them to accept and understand what I go through.

The eternal stigma I faced soon turned inward, and it was like carrying an invisible burden that grew heavier with each day. It wasn't the casual comments about "crazy people" from strangers that hurt the most. It was the pervasive sense of being seen as less than a normal person that cut deep into my self-worth. Soon, I started questioning my own worth and capabilities. If society saw me as a threat or a burden, did I have any value at all? I wondered if I was actually capable of making my own decisions and managing relationships. It took me quite a while to realize that all of it was lies I had internalized from the world around me.

One day, it just hit me. I remembered that I too, have a voice. I was 16 when I started my own blog. I began writing about my journey and my experiences and people read it. I wrote about my symptoms, my treatment, my happy times and my victories. People really liked it. They reached out to me sharing their own stories or expressing gratitude for throwing light at an often-misunderstood condition. Even strangers and people I barely knew reached out to me. I was being supported from unexpected places.

Of course, there have been challenges and setbacks. Not everyone is receptive, and some continue to hold on to their prejudices. I remind myself that change is slow and that every step forward is progress. Overcoming stigma is a never-ending process for both, myself and society. I continue to speak, write, and advocate hoping that future generations will face less prejudice and misunderstanding. Each time I speak out, I take another step toward a world where individuals with mental health conditions are seen, heard, and valued for who they truly are.

CHAPTER SEVEN

OH, I'M SO SORRY!

When you're a teenager living with something chronic, you lose all hope and will to function. And the only person who can bring that hope and life back into you is yourself. People will never know what to say to you. Trust me when I say this, the only thing they'll say is, "Oh, I'm so sorry you have to go through all of this". Meanwhile, I would be having the time of my life, living in my own bubble. When I was in the hospital, I would have two raspberry ice creams at once, I would play with my friends, I would be involved in group therapy and games, and all the little shenanigans. I didn't have to write exams. I was free. I was happy. And people didn't see that. Yes, of course, I have my struggles but my struggles are not my entire life. There is so much more to it than just that.

I'm sorry but I am not sorry for myself, and you don't have to be either. I have had people tell me that they could probably never go through what I go through but I want to say something. What I deal with is not necessarily worse than what you deal with. We have different lives and we can't measure the amount of suffering a person has. We all have our pain and we all have different ways of dealing with it. So you can't really tell if one person has suffered more than the other.

When you show pity towards someone who is dealing with an illness, you simply take away their power. You're supposed to empower them and show support. You need to give them strength because everybody else is just taking it away. Stop pitying, start empowering.

It's how we perceive things. I believe challenges are what make you strive toward growth. Challenges make you stronger. We're all going to die someday, some sooner than others. But we do have something in control and that is to live a life that we're proud of. Death is inevitable, might as well do something worthwhile when we're here. Otherwise, what is the point of living? We all have something beautiful to give to the world. And we can't keep waiting for the perfect timing to give. Health in itself will never make your life better. It is what you do with the health that you have rather than waiting for it to get better. There is no perfect circumstance.

My medications don't make me any better. They just help me function and help me deal with my symptoms. There is no magic. There is no better. Hence, I do what I can with whatever health I have. If I get better, that's great but I can't wait my entire life to get to a place where things are doable. They're doable even now. I just need to figure out how. And I will.

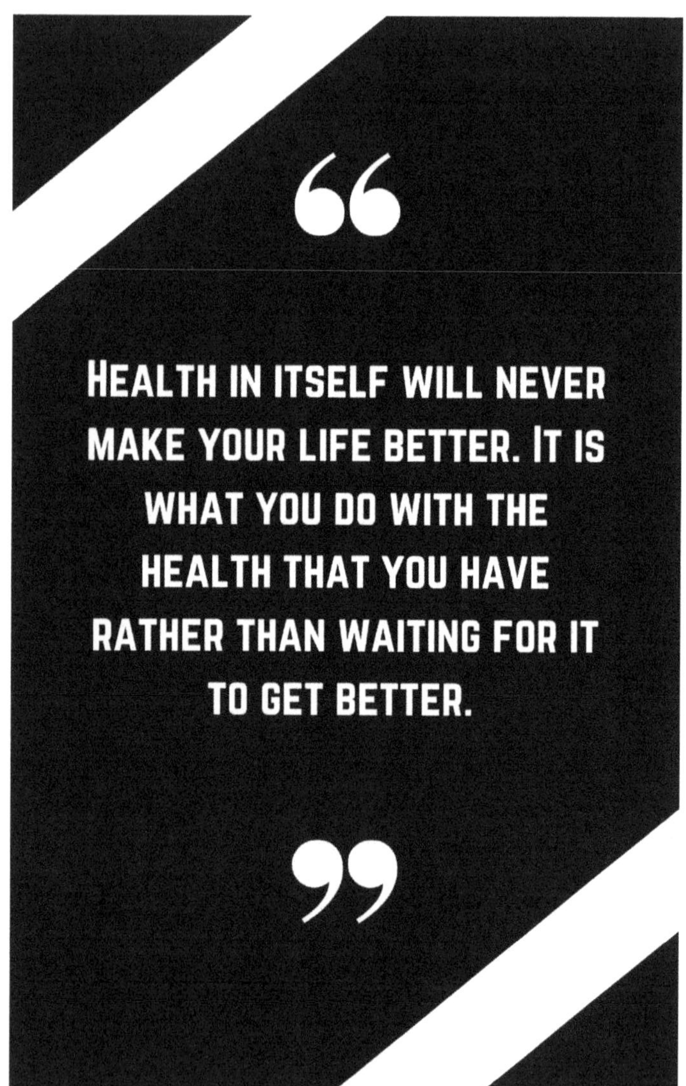
HEALTH IN ITSELF WILL NEVER MAKE YOUR LIFE BETTER. IT IS WHAT YOU DO WITH THE HEALTH THAT YOU HAVE RATHER THAN WAITING FOR IT TO GET BETTER.

CHAPTER EIGHT

How my Mind Affects my Body

This chapter is not generalized to people who have schizophrenia, dissociative disorders, anxiety, or depression. It is more specific towards me and how my mind hijacks my body at times. Few doctors say it might be due to dissociation, but the clear reason is still unknown.

So what exactly happens is, my body becomes stiff, making me incapable of movement. Or it may just be my legs that stop functioning. When something like this happens, I can't even lift my hand up to my head. I can't even move it and I'm usually bedridden. My mom helps me with every single thing. There are times when I cannot swallow any food or water. Sometimes, I can swallow water and liquids but most times, I can't.

There was this one time when I was in 10th or 11th grade and couldn't walk for months. I was then admitted to the psychiatric ward and had to go through intensive therapies and treatments after which I got slightly better. I had to relearn how to walk, one step at a time, just like a child would. I was confined to a wheelchair for a really long time. I had to take the help of a walker to start learning how to walk again.

I even randomly collapse sometimes, without any prior warning. I would be walking normally and the next second you'll find me on the floor. My breathing sometimes stops when I'm in the middle of an episode. I also have convulsions randomly, sometimes more than three times in just five minutes, each one leaving me more exhausted and disoriented than the last.

A mental illness can affect a person physically too. It can get severe as well. What we don't realize is when the headquarters is in trouble, it causes trouble to other parts of the body too.

Understanding this connection has been crucial for me. It's helped me recognize that my physical symptoms are not just isolated incidents but are directly linked to my mental health. This realization has been both empowering and daunting. On one hand, it means that by taking care of my mental health, I can potentially alleviate some of the physical symptoms. On the other hand, it also means that when my mental health takes a downturn, my body is likely to follow suit.

I've also had to educate myself about my condition and advocate for my needs. This means being proactive in my treatment, asking questions, and seeking out professionals who are knowledgeable and empathetic. It's a continuous learning process, and each episode teaches me something new about my mind and body.

Despite difficulties, I've discovered my inner power. Relearning to walk was one of the most difficult tasks I've ever faced, but it taught me patience and determination.

Every step I took, no matter how small, was an accomplishment. It served as a reminder that no matter how bad things felt, I had the strength to overcome.

These experiences have also helped me better comprehend the human body and mind. As a psychology student, I've learned firsthand how interrelated our mental and physical health are. This understanding has motivated my desire to help others and supported my decision to become a clinical psychologist.

CHAPTER NINE

My Love for Psychology

As a child, I always loved learning about why we do what we do. At the age of 12, I learned that there is a discipline that studies human mental processes and behaviour. Psychology was not taught as a subject at my school, but I was very much interested in it. After my 10th, I wanted to take up humanities and study psychology in pre-university.

Growing up, I was always curious about why people acted the way they did. I would observe my family, friends, and even strangers, trying to understand their motivations and emotions. This curiosity led me to read books about psychology and human behaviour, which opened up a whole new world for me. The more I learned, the more I wanted to know.

At twelve, most kids were engrossed in cartoons and video games, but I was drawn to documentaries and articles about psychology. I remember being fascinated by how different theories explained human behaviour, from Freud's psychoanalysis to Skinner's behaviourism. I started keeping a journal where I would jot down interesting observations and reflect on my thoughts. I would take online courses and learn from YouTube videos about the various aspects of psychology. This early involvement with psychology was not just a hobby; it felt like a calling.

I was also dealing with my anxiety and depression. I wanted to learn more about what was happening and why it was happening. Then I began dissociating and slipping into psychosis. Learning psychology was a leisure activity for me. I wanted to pursue psychology in my pre-university. But my parents told me to choose science because it had more scope, and they said that if I still liked psychology and had an interest in it 2 years later, I could take it up in college. That's exactly what I did. I was thrilled when I was accepted into a program that allowed me to study both psychology and journalism. Combining these two fields has been incredibly enriching, as it allows me to explore the human mind while also bettering my communication skills. I believe that being able to effectively communicate psychological concepts to a broader audience is crucial, especially when it comes to raising awareness about mental health issues.

Now, as I am finishing my second-year exams, I look back on what I've done so far with a sense of accomplishment and excitement for what has to come. My coursework has been both challenging and rewarding.

One of the most exciting aspects of my college experience has been the opportunity to engage in research. Working alongside teachers and friends on various research projects has been awesome. I have also written and presented three psychological research papers with one of my closest friends, Sneha. She writes her paper and I write mine. Then we present our own papers at a conference. I have presented all three papers with her. I presented two with Minnu Ma'am, who also is a well-wisher of mine.

I am particularly looking forward to my third year when I will finally get to dive into abnormal psychology. This is a subject that has always interested me adding to my personal experiences with mental health. Understanding the complexities of mental disorders and learning about the various treatment approaches will be invaluable as I pursue my goal of becoming a clinical psychologist. I am eager to learn about conditions such as schizophrenia, bipolar disorder, and anxiety disorders, and to explore how therapeutic interventions can make a difference in people's lives.

My ultimate goal is to become a clinical psychologist. I want to work with individuals who are struggling with mental health issues and provide them with the support and guidance they need to win over their challenges. My personal experiences have given me a unique perspective and empathy that I believe will help me in this role. I understand what it's like to feel overwhelmed by mental health issues, and I am committed to helping others find their way.

The path to becoming a clinical psychologist is not without its challenges. There are times when the weight of my academic responsibilities feels overwhelming, but my passion for the field keeps me motivated.

Additionally, my own mental health struggles have sometimes made it difficult to stay focused and productive. There have been days when anxiety and depression have threatened to derail my progress. However, I have learned to manage these challenges through therapy, self-care, and the support of my family and friends.

I want to continue learning and do my master's after my bachelor's degree. I know that the road ahead will be challenging, but I am ready to face whatever comes my way. I am also looking forward to internships and dealing with practical work in my final year.

Becoming a clinical psychologist is not just a career choice for me; it is a calling. It is something I am passionate about. With each year, my dedication grows stronger, and I am excited to see where this route will take me.

CHAPTER TEN

UNDERSTANDING TRIGGERS

There is always this interplay of reality and imagination, between what is, and what seems to be. One of the most difficult parts of living this life is dealing with triggers. A trigger is a person, place, thing, or situation that elicits an intense or unexpected emotional response or causes an individual to relive a past trauma. For me, one of the most persistent and terrifying triggers has been the colour red.

My struggle with the colour red goes back to a hallucination whose name is Sylvie. Sylvie has been a part of my life since the age of fourteen. She has red eyes and red hair. Her presence is both terrifying and intrusive. She appears without a warning and is not very nice when she does. The intensity of her presence is such that anything red- whether it's a red dress, a red car, or even a red flower- could trigger a reaction in me. It used to be much worse than it is now.

The fear of red was particularly pronounced at the age of fourteen. At that time, Sylvie's appearances were more frequent. My brain began associating the colour red with fear and danger. The sight of red would cause my heart to race, my palms to sweat, and my breathing to become shallow and rapid. These bodily reactions were my body's way of saying that I was in distress, even though logically, I knew there was no real danger.

This aversion to red colour affected my daily living. I avoided red clothing, red décor, and red things in general. My family and friends tried being supportive, but it was difficult for them to understand my irrational fear. For example, a simple trip to the grocery store could become a horrifying experience, if I encountered too many red items. Even in some instances where I couldn't control the colour red, I would have a difficult time.

Over the years, I've developed several coping mechanisms to manage my reaction to the colour red. One of the most effective strategies has been exposure therapy, a technique I learned during my sessions with a therapist. Exposure therapy basically involves gradually and repeatedly exposing oneself to the trigger in a controlled and safe environment which allows the brain to become desensitized to the fear response.

I began looking at pictures of red objects but in a calm and relaxed setting. This was very difficult and I could only manage a few seconds before losing it. However, with consistent practice, I was able to increase the duration. Eventually, I moved on to wearing red clothes and handling red objects for short periods of time. This gradual exposure to red objects reduced my sensitivity to the colour, although it didn't eliminate the trigger entirely.

Another important coping mechanism is mindfulness and grounding techniques. When I saw something red and felt the panic rise, I immediately focused on breathing and bringing my awareness to the present moment. I would go to someone whom I trust or touch a familiar object.

My family, friends, and therapists have all played a significant role in helping me with my triggers. They were initially puzzled by my reactions but even then, they were very understanding and supportive. They would even avoid wearing red or bringing red objects near me. More importantly, they provided a safe and non-judgmental space for me to talk about my fears.

Moreover, studying psychology has given me a deeper insight into the mechanisms of fear and anxiety. I've learned about the amygdala, the part of the brain responsible for processing emotions and triggering the fight-or-flight response. Understanding the biological basis of my reactions has made them more manageable (and less mysterious).

Being in a crowd or around too many people can be difficult. Being alone or not feeling included can also trigger me. Hence, I need to be given just that much attention so that I neither feel too excluded nor get overwhelmed by social situations. When I go out in social settings, I take at least one person whom I can trust. This helps me reduce anxiety.

Progress in managing triggers is rarely linear There have been times when I felt I was doing great, only to be set back by another unexpected incident. The setbacks can be discouraging but I've started to view them as a part of my progress. Every setback is just a step up.

Presently, I can deal with the colour red a lot better than before, but it still triggers me. I know I'll find my way through it, someday. Until then, wish me luck.

Triggers may never completely disappear, but with understanding, support, and effective coping strategies, they can be managed.

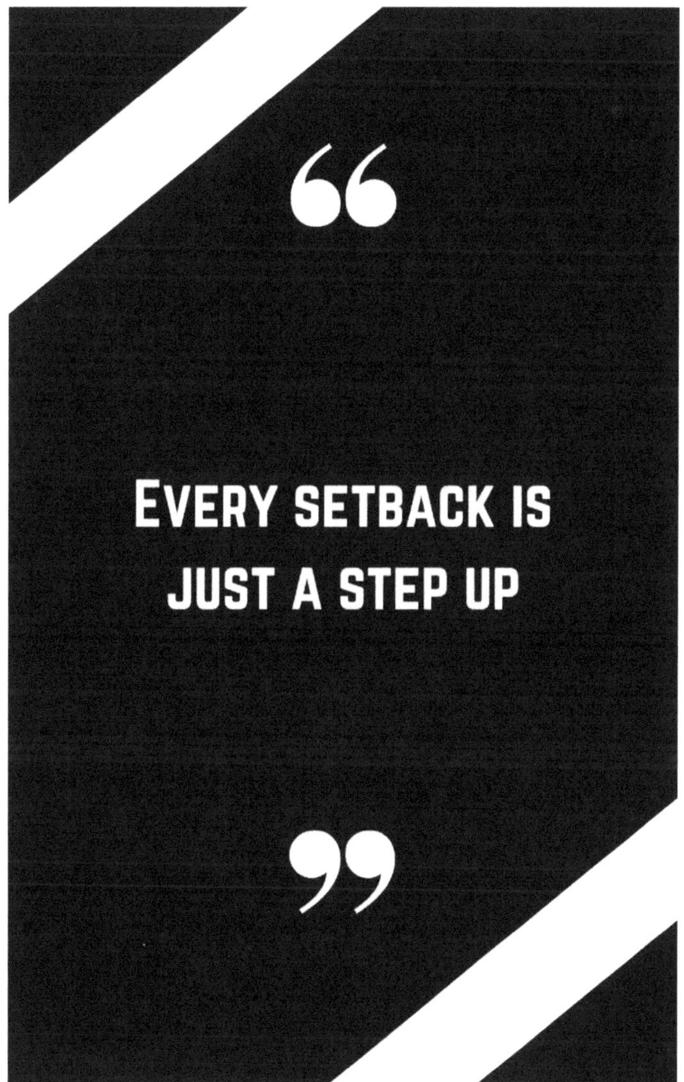
EVERY SETBACK IS
JUST A STEP UP

CHAPTER ELEVEN

SHIRO

Life is filled with twists and turns, and sometimes, the most profound lessons come from the most unlikely sources. In my case, one of the greatest teachers I've had is Shiro, my dog (more like a brother). This chapter is dedicated to Shiro, who is my source of inspiration and joy.

It was a lovely winter evening when Shiro first came into my life. I remember feeling a mix of excitement and nervousness as I held the tiny, trembling bundle of fur in my hands. Shiro is a Labrador Retriever, a breed known for its friendliness and loyalty.

Shiro was a very weak and frail puppy. His belly was bloated and he was severely underweight. His immunity was very low and he had to be on IV fluids. But even then, he was very lively. I couldn't bear seeing the vet piercing the needle through his arm. "He's very sick," the vet said gently, "I'm not sure if he'll make it through the next few weeks." Those words hit me like a ton of bricks. The thought of losing Shiro so soon after meeting him was unbearable.

Despite the serious prognosis, I made a decision that day. I was not going to give up on Shiro. I knew that he was in desperate need of love and care. I did everything in my control to give him the best life. I took him to the pet hospital every day for his treatments. Even if I were to lose him, I wasn't going to let him go without trying to bring him to a healthy state. This was the beginning of a beautiful journey of resilience and more importantly, mutual support.

The first few days were incredibly tough. Shiro's health was fragile, and every day felt like a battle. Feeding him was a challenge, as he had little appetite and often struggled to keep food down. I spent countless nights awake, monitoring him and ensuring he was comfortable. It was heartbreaking to see him in pain, but I knew that he needed me to be strong for him. My family and I tried our best to help our fellow family member.

As days turned into weeks, I could see him get better. There were tiny victories which brought lots of joy to my family and me. He would wag his tail at the sound of my voice and would play with him as though he wasn't going through anything. He had made it past his life expectancy and I was beyond happy. I was thrilled.

Watching Shiro fight his way through taught me resilience. Watching him fight against the odds and slowly regain strength made me realize the importance of hope. There were times when I felt overwhelmed and exhausted, but Shiro's spirit inspired me to keep going. He showed me that even during tough times, it is possible to keep going and pushing forward.

As his health got better, our bond grew stronger. He became my constant companion. He was by my side through thick and thin. His presence was enough to bring me joy and comfort. I had bad mental health days and he was always by my side. He could sense when I was feeling down and would snuggle up to me, offering silent reassurance. His unconditional love and support played a significant role in my life.

Shiro loves going outdoors. We would go on long walks, and enjoy the simple things in life. Shiro is a COVID baby so we couldn't do much outdoors. However, we had lots of fun indoors.

Shiro's way through not only transformed his life but also had a profound impact on mine. Caring for him taught me lots of things. It taught me patience, empathy, and resilience. He showed me that it's possible to overcome even the most challenging circumstances.

Shiro loves me regardless of my flaws and struggles. I have learned the value of loving and being loved without conditions or expectations.

Just like Shiro, I continue fighting each day. Shiro is my inspiration and will continue to be.

CHAPTER TWELVE

LIVING THROUGH PSYCHOSIS

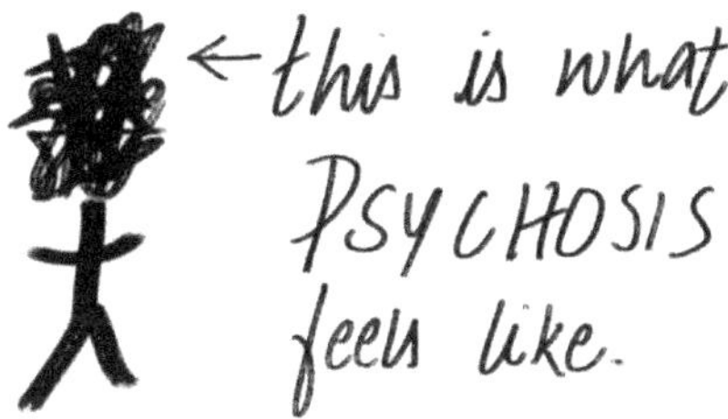

What do you think of when you think of the term 'psychosis'? I'll tell you what a lot of people think. Madness. Craziness. Confusion. Fear. Let's find out how far it's true. This chapter is an attempt to describe what psychosis feels like from the inside, from the perspective of someone who lives with it. This is psychosis from my point of view.

Psychosis is often subtle. It can start with small things- a sense of uneasiness, a feeling that something is off, or the sensation of being watched. For me, it begins with a heightened sensitivity to my surroundings. Colours are more vivid, sounds are louder, and my thoughts run through my head at the speed of light.

At first, these sensations might seem almost magical. But soon enough, the lines between what is real and what is not begin to blur. It's like a waking dream where the rules of logic don't even make sense. It seems like my education doesn't even matter at this point since nothing aligns with it.

One of the most characteristic features of psychosis is hallucinations. These can involve any of the senses, but for me, they are primarily visual and auditory. Seeing Sylvie, my hallucination with red eyes and red hair, is a haunting experience. She appears at the most unexpected moments, her presence always unsettling and sometimes terrifying.

When I see Sylvie or any other scary hallucination, it's not like seeing something imaginary or out of place. They feel just as real as the other people in the room. The rational part of my mind tells me that they're not there, but the emotional part says otherwise. Their appearance can trigger the worst of me. It can trigger fear and anxiety, especially when I'm alone or in a crowded place.

Auditory hallucinations are another common experience. Voices that aren't there whisper in my ear, they taunt me and are persistent. They might comment on my actions, criticize me, or tell me what to do. These voices can be so convincing that it becomes difficult to distinguish them from actual conversations. It's as if an invisible presence is constantly talking to you, and you're never quite sure who's real and who's not.

Delusions happen to be another feature of psychosis. These are strong beliefs that are held firmly despite clear evidence that what I'm believing is not true. For me, delusions revolve around paranoia. They are incredibly convincing. The feeling of being watched or followed is not just a vague suspicion; it feels just as real as the ground beneath me. My mind can make sense of the most random things. If I see patterns in something, I interpret them as signs and messages. I also feel like people can see what I see and hear what I hear, which is quite creepy if you give it a thought.

The challenge with delusions is that they are self-reinforcing. The more you believe in them, the more evidence you seem to find to support them. It creates a closed loop of thought that is incredibly difficult to break out of.

One of the most disorienting aspects of psychosis is disorganized thinking. Thoughts come in bits and pieces, jumping from one idea to another with no logical connection.

For me, this manifests as a rapid flow of thoughts that I can't control. One moment, I'm thinking about a conversation I had earlier and the next, I'm obsessing over a random memory from years ago. It's difficult to focus on any single task, and even simple conversations can become confusing and overwhelming.

I might start talking about one thing and suddenly veer off into a completely unrelated topic. It can be frustrating for both me and the people around me. They might think I'm not making sense or that I'm not listening, but the reality is that my mind is simply unable to stay on track.

Psychosis is not just a mental experience; it's deeply emotional too. There are times I feel insane amounts of fear and intense loneliness as if I'm cut off from everyone around me.

It might also be joy. Sometimes I'm way too happy about the randomest of things. Then my mood swings.

The mood swings are exhausting. They bring down my energy and stability. It's like living in a storm and that storm is passing, shifting, and changing, but never really ending.

Medication plays a crucial role in managing my psychosis, but it's not without its challenges. Finding the right medication and dosage is a complex process that involves a lot of trial and error. Some medications can help reduce the intensity of my symptoms, but they often come with side effects that can be difficult to manage.

For example, some medications make me feel drowsy and lethargic, while others can cause weight gain or other physical issues. There's also the constant worry about becoming dependent on medication or developing tolerance over time. Despite these challenges, medication remains an essential part of my treatment plan. My doctor and I are still finding the perfect balance and combination of medications that can help me, but nothing seems to work sometimes.

Living with psychosis is a continuous journey. There are good days and bad days, moments of clarity and times of confusion. But through it all, I've learned that recovery is possible. It's not about eliminating all symptoms or becoming "normal." Instead, it's about finding ways to manage the condition and live a fulfilling life despite it.

Recovery means different things to different people. For me, it's about building resilience, developing coping strategies, and maintaining a strong support network. It's about finding joy in the small moments and celebrating the progress I have made.

Hope is a powerful force. It's the belief that things can get better, that there is light at the end of the tunnel. Even in the darkest moments, holding onto hope provides the strength to keep moving forward.

Hope is not about unrealistic optimism or denying the challenges we face. It's about acknowledging the difficulties and believing in the possibility of positive change. It's about finding meaning and purpose in our experiences and using them as a source of strength.

Through my own experiences, I've learned that it's possible to live a meaningful and fulfilling life with psychosis.

> **HOPE IS NOT ABOUT UNREALISTIC OPTIMISM OR DENYING THE CHALLENGES WE FACE. IT'S ABOUT ACKNOWLEDGING THE DIFFICULTIES AND BELIEVING IN THE POSSIBILITY OF POSITIVE CHANGE.**

CHAPTER THIRTEEN

TO DIE IS HUMAN

To die is human. But to live is a choice we make. I have something to say. Something, I never thought I'd tell the world. It's the fact that I have attempted suicide quite a few times. The thing I'm grateful for is that I've survived all those times. There are times I found myself in drug overdose situations and other circumstances which I do not wish to discuss here. But the most important thing is I found my way out.

What I realize now being alive, is that I'm glad I didn't die. I don't want to die. Because there is so much that a human being is capable of and we don't realize that until we're in the fangs of death. There is so much of value that I want to give to the world and I often feel like I'm running out of time. I'm already twenty and I feel I haven't done enough. I feel I haven't achieved enough.

Yes, we're all going to die someday. All of us, at different times. It's nothing to be scared of. What you should be scared of is not leaving a mark on this earth, of not giving something valuable to this earth. We all have something to give and people who have suffered too have something to give. In fact, they have the most beautiful things to give. We don't seem to understand the fact that we don't have a lot of time.

There are studies that say people with schizophrenia tend to have a life span of 10-20 years shorter than those of normal human beings. And that fact scares me because maybe, just maybe, if the study is true, I've got less time to do my part than others. My purpose, my thing to give is something that makes other people not want to die. I want the world to have better mental health so there are fewer deaths due to suicide. Every forty seconds a life is lost due to suicide. Isn't that disheartening? Let me also get something straight. People who commit suicide or those who have attempted suicide aren't cowards. It's not that they don't want to face life. They are pushed to come to a point like this.

We are human beings and we are incredibly capable of doing so many things. Let's put our brains to some use because nobody else will give our part to this world. You have got to do your part. We need to live lives that we're proud of. And no matter what you do, and how much you give, you will always feel like it isn't enough. That is when you'll know that you have given something of yourself.

There was a pivotal moment in my life that made me reconsider my existence. It wasn't a grand epiphany but rather a series of small realizations that accumulated over time. It began with the understanding that my pain was valid, but it did not define me. The first step towards healing was acknowledging that my life had value beyond my struggles.

One of the most profound realizations was discovering my purpose. Everyone talks about finding their purpose in life, but for someone battling mental illness, this can seem like an impossible task. However, it was through my darkest of times that I began to understand my calling. I realized that my purpose was to help others who were struggling like me. I wanted to use my experiences to inspire hope and to show that recovery and happiness were possible.

Another critical aspect of my journey was building a support system. Isolation can be one of the most damaging aspects of mental illness. I learned that reaching out for help wasn't a sign of weakness but a step towards strength. Friends, family, and therapists became my lifeline. They provided a safe space where I could express my fears and anxieties without judgment. Surrounding myself with people who understood and supported me made a significant difference in my growth process.

I also had to redefine what success meant to me. Society often equates success with tangible achievements, such as wealth, status, or career milestones. But for me, success meant something different. It meant waking up each day and choosing to fight. It meant finding joy in the little things and appreciating the moments of peace amidst the chaos. Success was no longer about external validation but about internal contentment and growth.

My experiences have also led me to become an advocate for mental health awareness. I realized that one of the biggest obstacles to mental health is the stigma associated with it. By sharing my story, I hope to challenge these stigmas and encourage others to seek help without shame. Advocacy has become a way for me to give back and ensure that no one else feels as isolated as I once did.

Gratitude became another powerful tool in my life. Even during the toughest times, I forced myself to find things to be grateful for. It could be something as simple as a cloudy day (I don't like the sun) or a kind word from a friend. Focusing on gratitude shifted my perspective from what was wrong in my life to what was right. It reminded me that even in the midst of suffering, there were moments of beauty and grace.

Now, as I look forward to the future, I am filled with a sense of purpose and passion. My experiences have shaped me into a more empathetic and resilient person. I am committed to continuing my education in psychology and becoming a clinical psychologist. I want to help others go through their own mental health journeys and find the strength to live fulfilling lives. My career aspirations are not just about professional success but about making a meaningful impact on the world.

We all have a limited time here. Let's make it worthwhile.

> **What you should be scared of is not leaving a mark on this earth, of not giving something valuable to this earth.**

CHAPTER FOURTEEN

WRITING AND RAISING FUNDS

I used to write in my diary when I was a child. I used to pour out my thoughts, dreams and wishes onto paper. It was comforting to see the ink bleed through the pages and feel the friction of the pen's nib on the paper. Not only that, I liked expressing myself through writing. Even though nobody read it (at least I hope nobody did), it was an outlet for me. I felt free and relaxed once all the thoughts were out in my diary.

When I was eight years old, I handwrote a book. I carefully cut out A4 size sheets in half and decorated each page with markers, stickers, and glitter. The book was called "Nothing is Impossible ". It said nothing is impossible if you commit to it. At that age, that is what came to my mind. I wrote about my experiences with rock climbing and how I climbed all the way to the top. I stuck pictures and made it look pretty.

I grew a little older and at the age of fifteen, I started a website using wix.com. It was a blog website, I began writing blogs on that website. It was called something like "Create Clarity". There, I would post about my life and how

I was dealing with it.

Then, in the eleventh grade, I felt that there was very little help for people who live with psychosis. 1 out of 10 people who live with schizophrenia take their own lives. I wanted to do something that I could, to help people living with psychosis. I started a small fundraiser and called it "The Psych Place Foundation" and I raised a lot of money that came from people whom I knew and whom I didn't know. Funds started coming in from the most unexpected sources. I then donated the funds to NIMHANS.

Writing was my way through. I found solace in writing. Random people reached out to me with their stories after reading my blogs. After getting into college, I started another blog and deleted the previous one, because obviously, I am Priti and Priti wants perfection. Anyway, I wrote about more things and people read that too and reached out to me. The blog is still active. It's called "Wholeheartedly, Priti" on Blogger. That's how I sign my name, that's how I end my blogs, that's how I write my letters. That's just how it is. It is like my domain.

At the age of nineteen, my first book was published. It's called, "Finding Clarity in the Chaos". It's not as detailed as this book. That book was very little about my life. This book is more personalized to me. I'll be honest, I'm not being completely, totally, entirely transparent while writing this book. All that I have written is true but I haven't included my self-harm and suicide attempts in detail because it can be triggering to some people.

I still continue writing my blogs. I also do some content writing for my college events and all that. So I keep writing here and there, and keep living my laif as I get it.

THIS IS

from, me ♡ to, you

CHAPTER FIFTEEN

WORDS HAVE POWER

You must have heard people say, "I'm depressed", "I'm so OCD", "I'm autistic" etc. when they aren't even diagnosed with those disorders. You might be someone who has said this too. The problem is a part of the world views mental illnesses as a joke. You might think, it's not wrong to say it. I say it's not right!

Using these words as adjectives does not make you any different from the people who are actually suffering from these illnesses. Hence, it's being normalized. How are they supposed to seek help if people around them are normalizing having depression, OCD, or autism?

Even when my friends tell me that they're in depression, the first thing I ask them is whether they have serious symptoms or if they've been diagnosed. The answer that comes out is no.

It's disheartening because these terms carry a lot of weight and represent real conditions. For those of us who live with mental illnesses, hearing others casually toss around these labels can feel invalidating and dismissive. It lessens our struggles and contributes to the stigma that surrounds mental health.

When people casually say they are "depressed" because they had a bad day, or claim to be "OCD" because they like things neat, it distorts the public's understanding of these conditions. Clinical depression is more than just feeling sad; it's a persistent and pervasive state of hopelessness, fatigue, and disinterest in life. Obsessive-compulsive disorder involves intrusive, distressing thoughts and repetitive behaviours that are performed to satisfy anxiety, not simply a preference for orderliness. In fact, there are so many types of OCD.

Autism, too, is a complex neurological condition that affects how individuals perceive the world and interact with others. It's not merely being socially awkward or having a specific interest; it's a spectrum of conditions that require understanding and support.

When the severity and reality of these conditions are downplayed, it becomes harder for those genuinely affected to be taken seriously. It can discourage them from seeking help, fearing they'll be seen as exaggerating or attention-seeking.

It's essential to differentiate between casual expressions of mood or behaviour and actual clinical conditions. This differentiation helps validate the experiences of those with mental illnesses.

When someone says they're "depressed," it's important to listen and ask questions to understand their state of mind better. Instead of dismissing their feelings, we should encourage them to seek professional help if needed. Similarly, when someone claims to have OCD or autism traits, gently educating them about the true nature of these conditions can be helpful.

If you've ever used these terms casually, it's not too late to change. Reflect on how your words might affect others and consider how you can speak more accurately and sensitively. Educating yourself about mental health conditions can also help you communicate more effectively and supportively.

Let's remember that our words have power. They can either contribute to stigma and misunderstanding or elevate empathy and support. By choosing our words carefully and with compassion, we can make a positive difference in the lives of those affected by mental illnesses.

So next time you catch yourself or someone else using mental health terms casually, take a moment to reflect and educate. It might seem like a small step, but it's one that can have a significant impact. Together, we can help reduce stigma, foster understanding, and create a world where it's okay to seek help and talk about mental health openly and respectfully.

CHAPTER SIXTEEN

A Random Little Something

Hey you,

We all have our own unique way of living life (let's call it "laif" because I like it like that). My way of living may not be the same as yours, and that's totally okay. One size does NOT fit all. I can't tell you how to live your life, but I can share some things for you to consider.

One thing to remember is that we don't have forever. None of us will be around forever. We never know when we'll make our last phone call or take our final breath. We don't know how much time we have left here. We don't know when we'll be gone. All that we have sometimes, is just a single day. The thing is we take laif for granted. Don't even get me started on how people take reality for granted. I hope that's a whole other chapter. You have got to live each day like it is your last.

My hallucinations threaten me all the time with death. That's what has made me value laif more. If we'll all be gone, what should really matter most? The answer is simple. The time that you're here matters most. There were times I overdosed when I was dissociated. So, I didn't really know what I was doing. And when I was lying there in the hospital, with an NG tube, I was afraid that I'll die. Nothing has ever scared me more than that.

In one of the previous chapters, I said that death is inevitable. Do you know what else is inevitable? Laif! Laif is just as inevitable as death. You didn't ask for your laif. You got it. Hence, it is a gift. Laif is a beautiful, magnificent, wonderful thing. You don't want to lose it.

And before you say, "Priti, I know all this. Why are you telling me?" I have an answer. I am completely aware of the fact that you know it. But sometimes, we forget things whilst knowing them. Therefore, Priti here (that's me) is just reminding you. Because what's remembered, lives.

And if you're fighting suicidal urges, know that I'm proud of you. There is a laif for you to live, enjoy, suffer, and cry. Laif in itself is a good enough thing to convince yourself to keep fighting.

As they say, laif moves pretty fast. If you don't stop and look around once in a while, you could miss it. And if you ever feel lonely, know that all of us creatures have one thing at least in common. We share the same sky. I'm glad I share the same sky with you.

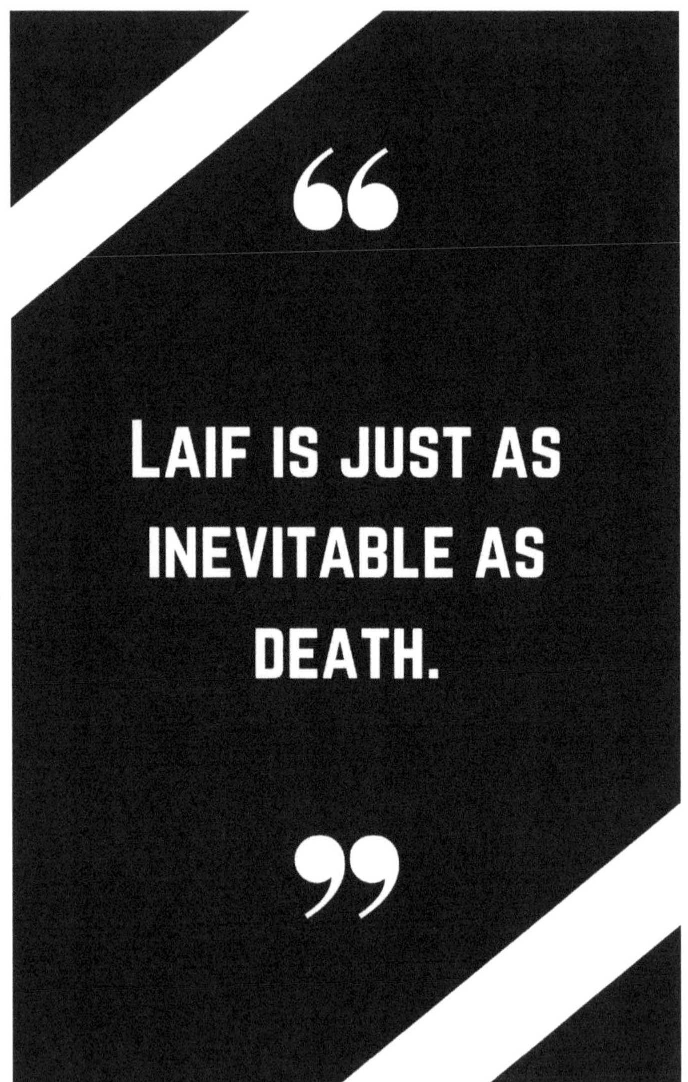
"
LAIF IS JUST AS
INEVITABLE AS
DEATH.
"

CHAPTER SEVENTEEN

IS IT REALLY OKAY NOT TO BE OKAY?

Life is complex and it has its own turbulence. It comprises joy, sorrow, triumph, defeat and so much more. In all this, there is this notion that we've found. It's this mantra: It's okay not to be okay. It is a sort of reassurance that it's alright to experience mental and emotional struggles. But is it really okay not to be okay?

I know that in my first book, I've written a chapter saying it is, in fact, okay not to be okay. I haven't changed my say much. In my view, it is okay not to be okay, but with an important caveat. That is, you need to pull yourself together eventually. Being emotionally unwell is a part of the human experience, but remaining in that state indefinitely is not conducive to a fulfilling life. Let's see why being not okay is okay, and how essential it is to commit to pulling yourself back together.

"Pain is inevitable. Suffering is optional." — Haruki Murakami

Human beings are inherently emotional creatures. We feel deeply, love passionately, and hurt profoundly. Our capacity to experience a broad spectrum of emotions is what makes us human. There will be times when we are not okay, and that's a natural part of life. Grief, disappointment, heartbreak, and failure are all experiences that contribute to our emotional landscape.

So, it is okay not to be okay. It's just not okay to stay that way. The first step towards healing is acknowledging that we aren't okay. Living in denial will only lead to more significant problems down the line. When we admit to others that we're struggling, we take the first step towards recovery. This acknowledgement is essential for self-awareness and emotional intelligence. It is a recognition that we're vulnerable and vulnerability is a strength, not a weakness.

Accepting that we are not okay, even temporarily, can be a powerful step towards healing. It allows us to process our emotions fully and authentically. This acceptance can provide the space needed to understand what we are feeling and why. However, it is crucial to remember that this acceptance should be temporary. Emotional pain is a signal that something is wrong, and it often requires action to address the underlying issues.

Never be pleased with your suffering. Prolonged distress can lead to a state of learned helplessness, where we begin to believe that we are powerless to change the situation. This mindset can hinder us from taking the necessary steps towards betterment.

"Healing takes time, and asking for help is a courageous step." — Mariska Hargitay

The first step of healing is the hardest: asking for help. If you can't do it alone, it's okay to lean on somebody for help.

Self-compassion is a critical component of healing. When we are not okay, it's easy to fall into a pattern of self-criticism and negative self-talk. However, it's essential to treat ourselves with the same kindness and understanding that we would offer to a friend. Self-compassion involves recognizing our humanity, understanding that suffering is a part of the human experience, and offering ourselves grace and forgiveness. So talk to yourself how you would talk to a friend.

Resilience is the ability to bounce back from adversity, and it is a skill that can be developed over time. Building resilience can include cultivating a positive mindset, developing coping strategies, and developing a support network. It also requires a commitment to self-care and maintaining a healthy balance in life. Resilience doesn't mean that we won't face challenges, but it does mean that we will be better equipped when they arise. So fall seven times, stand up eight.

Hope is a powerful force that can sustain us through difficult times. It is the belief that things can and will get better, even when we are in the midst of pain. Cultivating hope involves focusing on the positive aspects of our lives, setting goals for the future, and maintaining a sense of purpose. Hope provides the motivation to keep moving forward, even when the path is challenging.

In my own life, I have faced numerous emotional challenges. Living with schizophrenia and other mental health issues has been a path marked by highs and lows. There have been times when I was not okay, and I had to learn to accept that it was part of my experience. However, I also had to commit to pulling myself together and taking action to improve my situation.

One of the most valuable lessons I've learned is that it's okay not to be okay, but it's essential to strive for better mental health. This means seeking help, building resilience, and maintaining hope. It also means being kind to myself and recognizing that healing is a journey, not a destination.

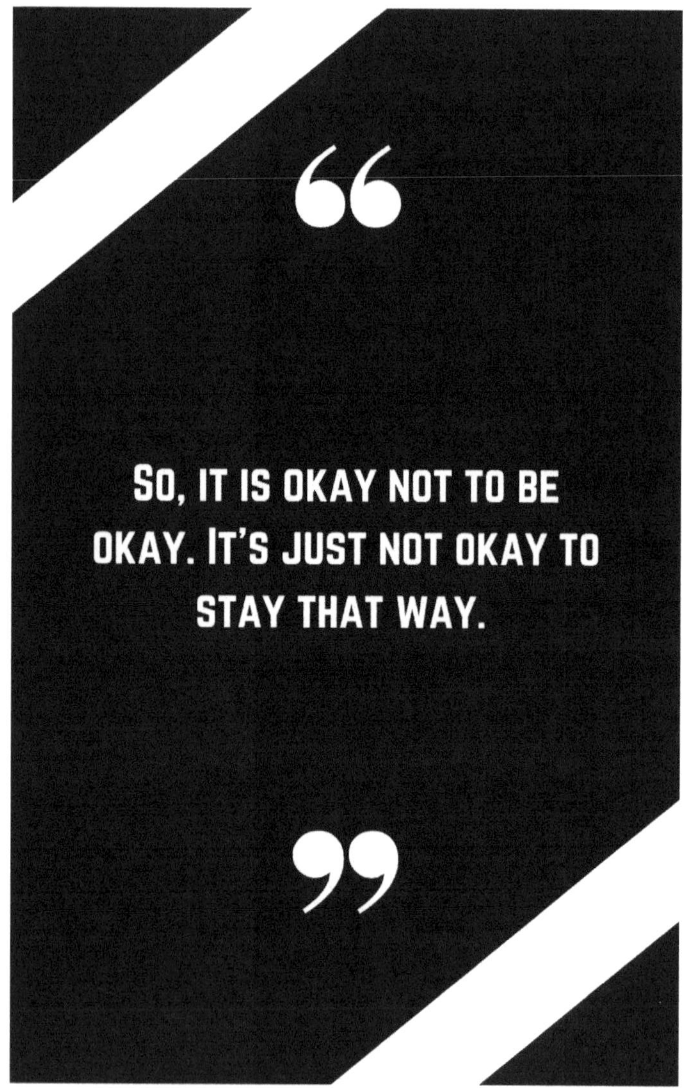

CHAPTER EIGHTEEN

A Reason? Is That It?

If I had to describe myself as a student, I'd say I'm pretty above average. I have the highest CGPA in my class. But my CGPA has been falling. In the first semester, I had a CGPA of 9.54. It then came down to 9.53 in my second semester. You'd say that's just 0.01 less. What's the big deal? Then my CGPA dropped to 9.46. Currently, I am taking my finals for the fourth semester and I don't know how the numbers will change this time. But I told myself that the universe is giving me a sign to stop focusing too much on grades because marks are not everything. And academic validation (that I seek) is not everything. I just couldn't find a valid reason. So, I told myself, "Priti, just trust the process. It's all happening for a reason." and I moved on.

My point being, how many times have you said that to yourself? That everything happens for a reason? I mean, is it true? Or do we find reasons for all that happens to us? We do that just to convince ourselves and to make ourselves feel better. You'll find reasons when laif gives you any circumstances. We fill our lives with bucketloads of sad lies.

It's a very short chapter, but that's all I want to say. Everything does not happen for a reason. We find reasons for all that happens.

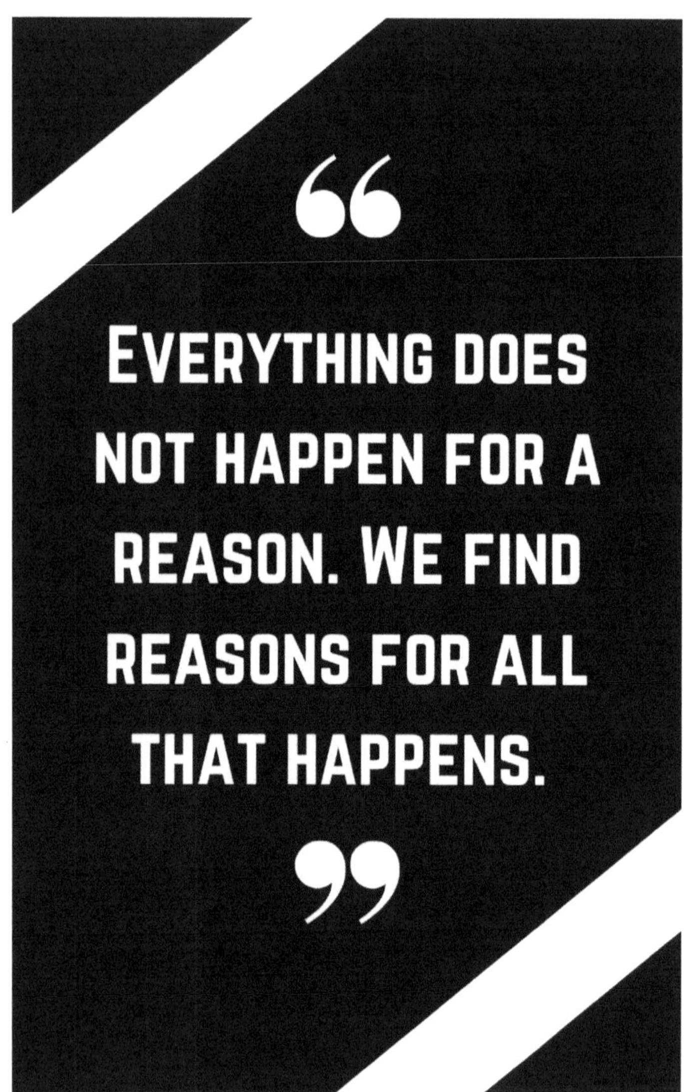
EVERYTHING DOES NOT HAPPEN FOR A REASON. WE FIND REASONS FOR ALL THAT HAPPENS.

(Maybe, my POV)

A Message Of Hope

If you're somebody who is struggling, I want you to know that I'm proud of you for fighting. I assure you that there is light at the end of the tunnel. This darkness won't last forever, I promise. Don't be afraid to ask for help. So, just give it your all and keep going no matter what. You have got this.

Wholeheartedly,
Priti

What People Have To Say About "finding Clarity In The Chaos"

Here's what a few people have said about my first book, "Finding Clarity in the Chaos".

Hey Priti
Hope you remember me!!!
Btw I just finished reading your book and I'm so touched tbh it's very inspiring..
And yes ppl never take mental health seriously..when i was taking treatment I met some ppl who told me I was faking things but only I knew what I was going through.. i am really proud of uh for trying to change the mindset of people..
I know we were good frnds in hospital but i never knew wht uh were going through and what was ur illness. Ps: I'm not pitying you but after reading this book I just feel like I know you better thn before. hope you are doing fine..and tbh I'm really happy for the person uh have become.. And look at uh....uh have really changed a lot..when I saw ur recent picture it felt like I'm seeing new version of uh who is happier thn before..
And i would say I'm kinda emotionally attached to this book now mostly becoz I can kinda relate things and tbh it's one of the best books.
Sending you lots of love

I ordered your book, read it and am mighty impressed by your presentation, clarity of thought and expression. Great job and well done

15:16

Hello Superstar, it's a proud moment to see your book launch. You know you have a lot to give to this world and make it a better place, we all know you do! Keep on your journey and keep shining! Lots of love Sis!

21:35

⭐⭐⭐⭐⭐ **A story of true warrior who don't know giving up.....**
Reviewed in India on 19 May 2024

This is a great book by a very young lady Preeti known for abundance of maturity, acceptance and tons of inspiration.. A true story of struggling teen for peace of mind and happiness.. This book brings a lot of confidence to teens especially who are floating in dreams and unable to accept reality.. So guys gift your children or anyone who wants to be think mature enough about life. I thank Preeti for the wonderful book and God bless you Preeti with abundance of happy and healing stay bless keep writing and inspiring...

WHAT PEOPLE HAVE TO SAY ABOUT "FINDING CLARITY IN THE CHAOS"

★★★★☆ **Thought provoking**

Reviewed in India on 3 November 2023

Verified Purchase

Here a book with many takeaways, but biggest one is to respect all, thank God for one's life n enjoy life to the Max, do good to all without being judgemental

★★★★★ **An amazing book by an amazingly strong person!**

Reviewed in India on 2 November 2023

Verified Purchase

A beautifully penned perspective on what one goes through during mental illness. Priti is an inspiration to many.

★★★★★ **you may have a chaotic life for many reasons but finding your way out is important**

Reviewed in India on 3 October 2023

Verified Purchase

The book is a very good attempt by a teenager to understand herself and her illness. Also wanting to help similar others who live with the victim mentality throughout their lives.

★★★★★ **Proud of you priti for not giving up yourself**

Reviewed in India on 25 September 2023

An amazing book which really speaks about finding the clarity in the chaos.The Book really gives you an insight into how the mental health illness works in really rather than adding all the colours to make it as a source of entertainment.I am also really proud of the priti who never stopped trying and always fighting back alone.Thank you priti for an amazing book.

www.ingramcontent.com/pod-product-compliance
Lightning Source LLC
Chambersburg PA
CBHW040126150726
48005CB00015B/2379